Draw What?

A Doodling, Drawing and Colouring Book

There are lots of doodles to do!

What designs can You add to the beach towels and umbrellas?

What can you add to the socks to turn them into puppets?

What are the passengers doing on the bus?

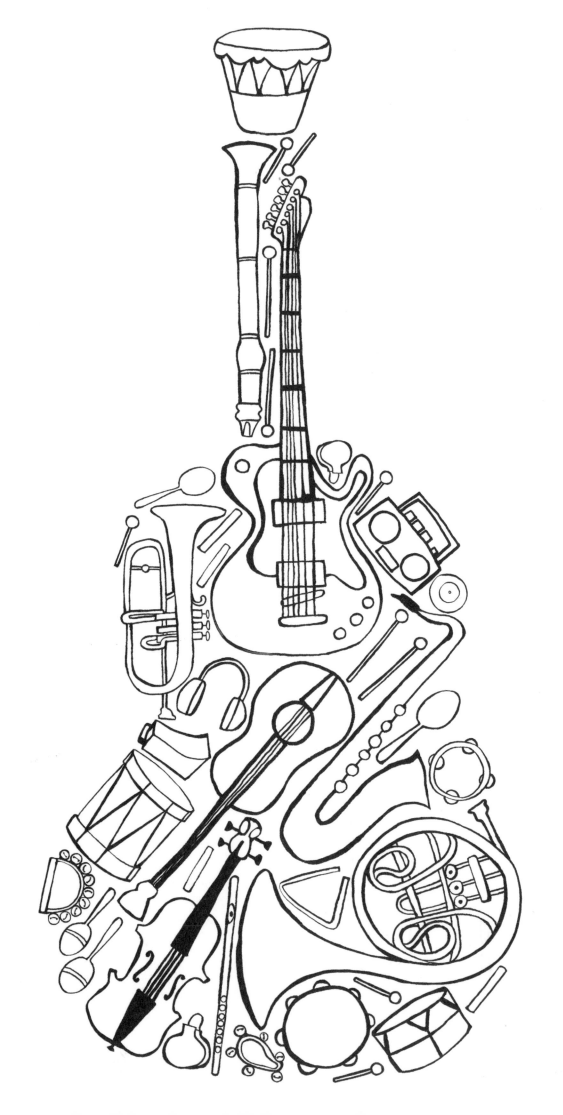

What crazy characters can you create from these boiled eggs?

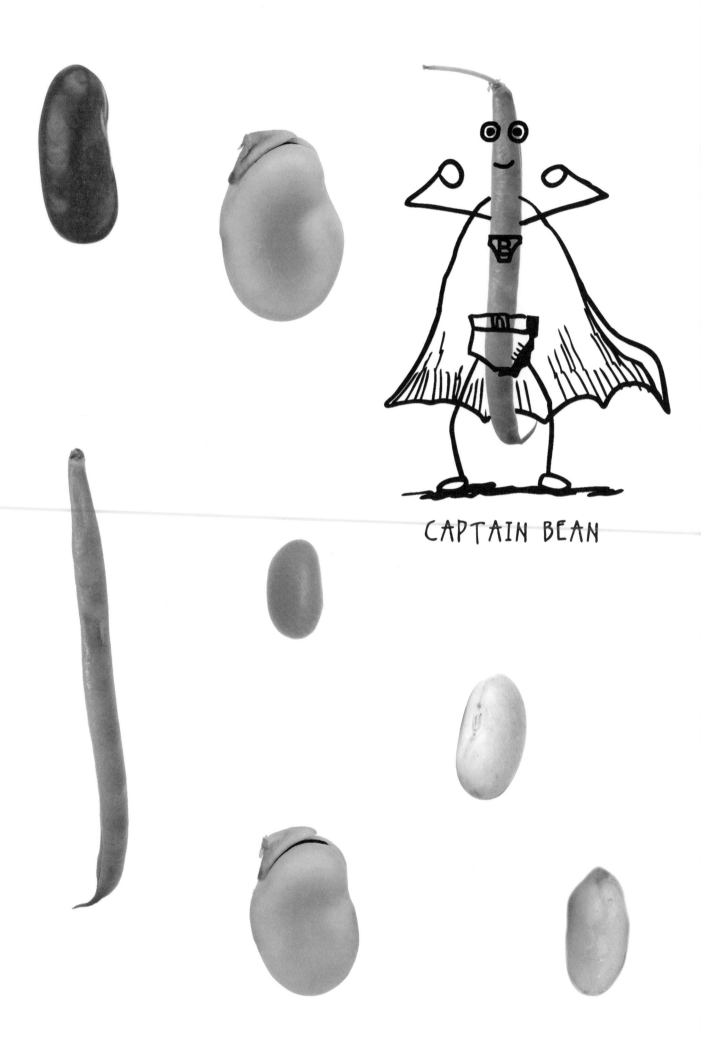

CAPTAIN BEAN

What kooky characters can you create out of these beans?

What types of birds are sitting in the tree?

What is going on in this apartment building?

What patterns can you add to these origami cranes?

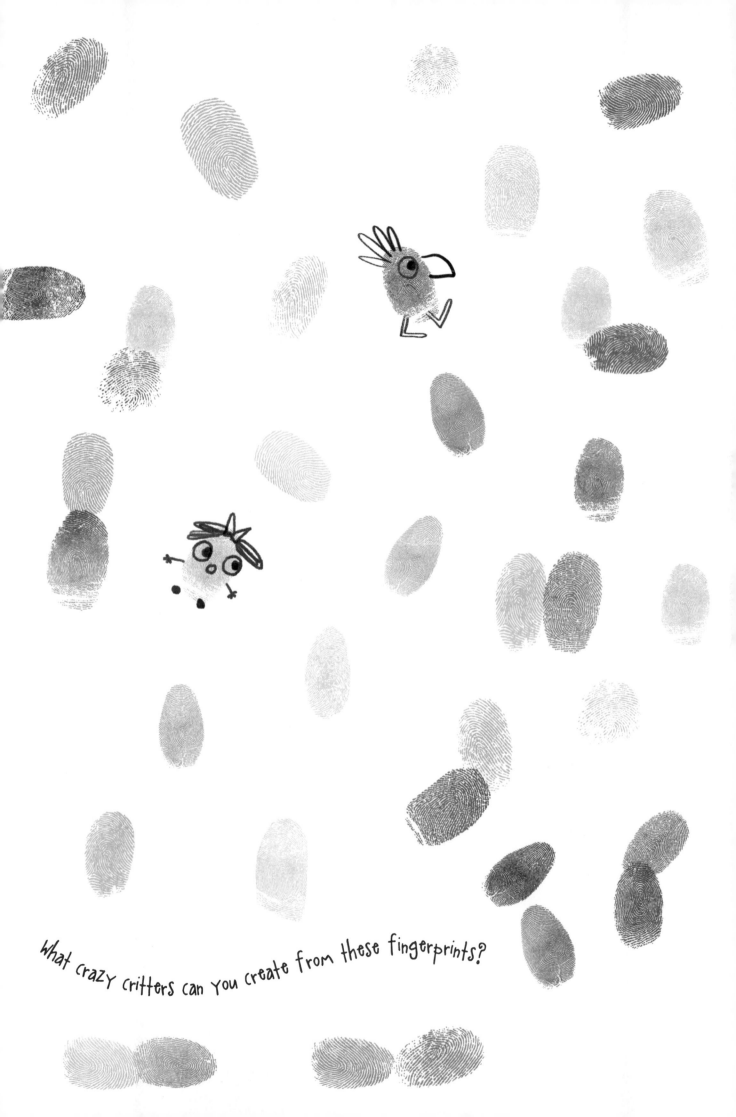

What crazy critters can You create from these fingerprints?

What has naughty Timmy drawn on the old family photos?

What do the dragon's scales look like?

What cool patterns and colours can you add to the sneakers?

What is hanging on the Christmas tree?

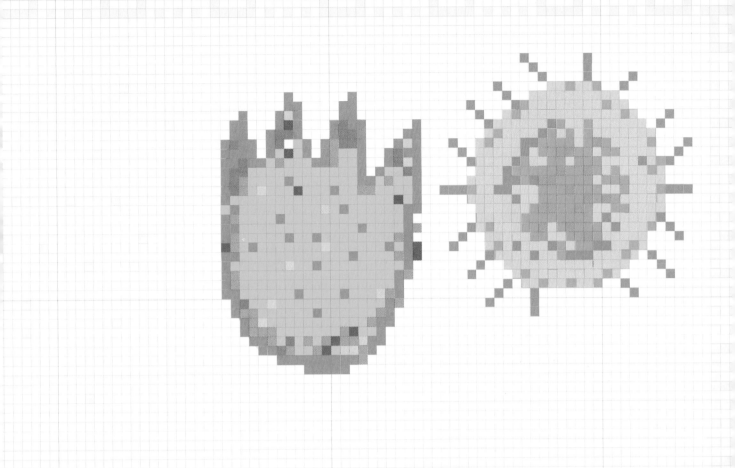

What flowers
can you create
by colouring in
the squares?

What decorations can you add to the Russian dolls?

What patterns and colours can you add to these giraffes?

What is Santa carrying in his sleigh?

what is happening in this prehistoric scene?

What costumes and make-up are these clowns wearing?

what is in the harbour?

What did the fisherman catch and what got away?

What can be found underground?

what amazing paper planes can you fly?

What wild hairstyles do these music fans have?

What crazy rockstar make-up can you add to the audience at the gig?

What sort of animals can you turn these circles into?

What are the superheroes and villains up to in this city?

What costumes are your superheroes wearing?

What do your fairies and their cottages look like?

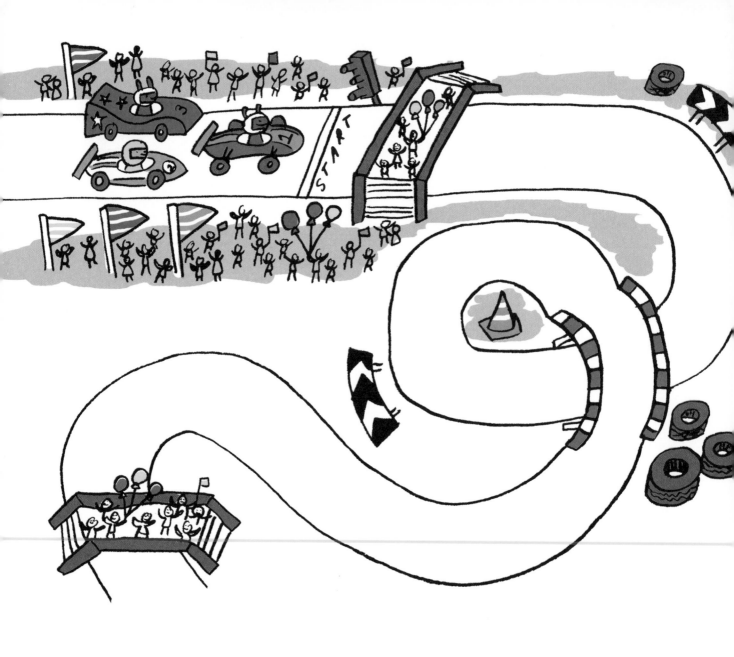

START

what is happening at the race track?

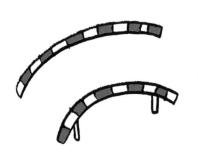

What will your pirate island look like

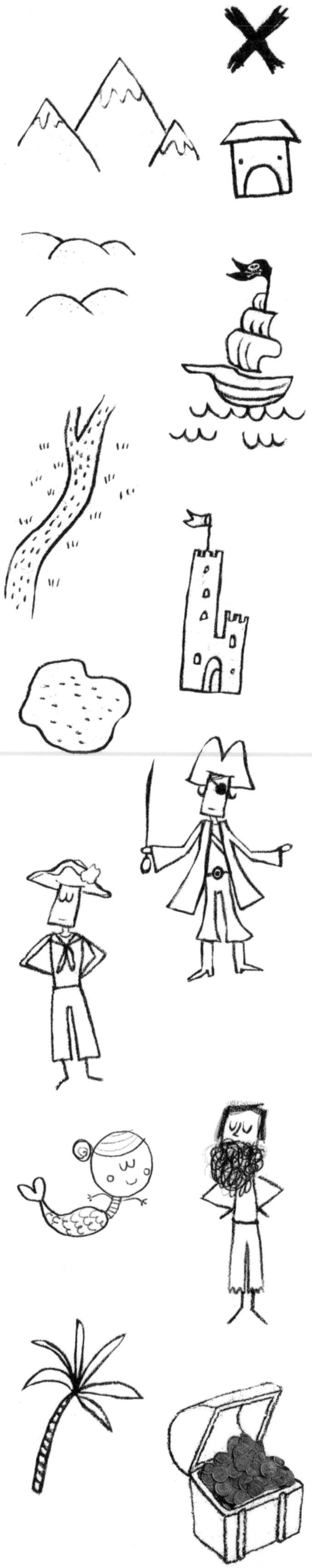

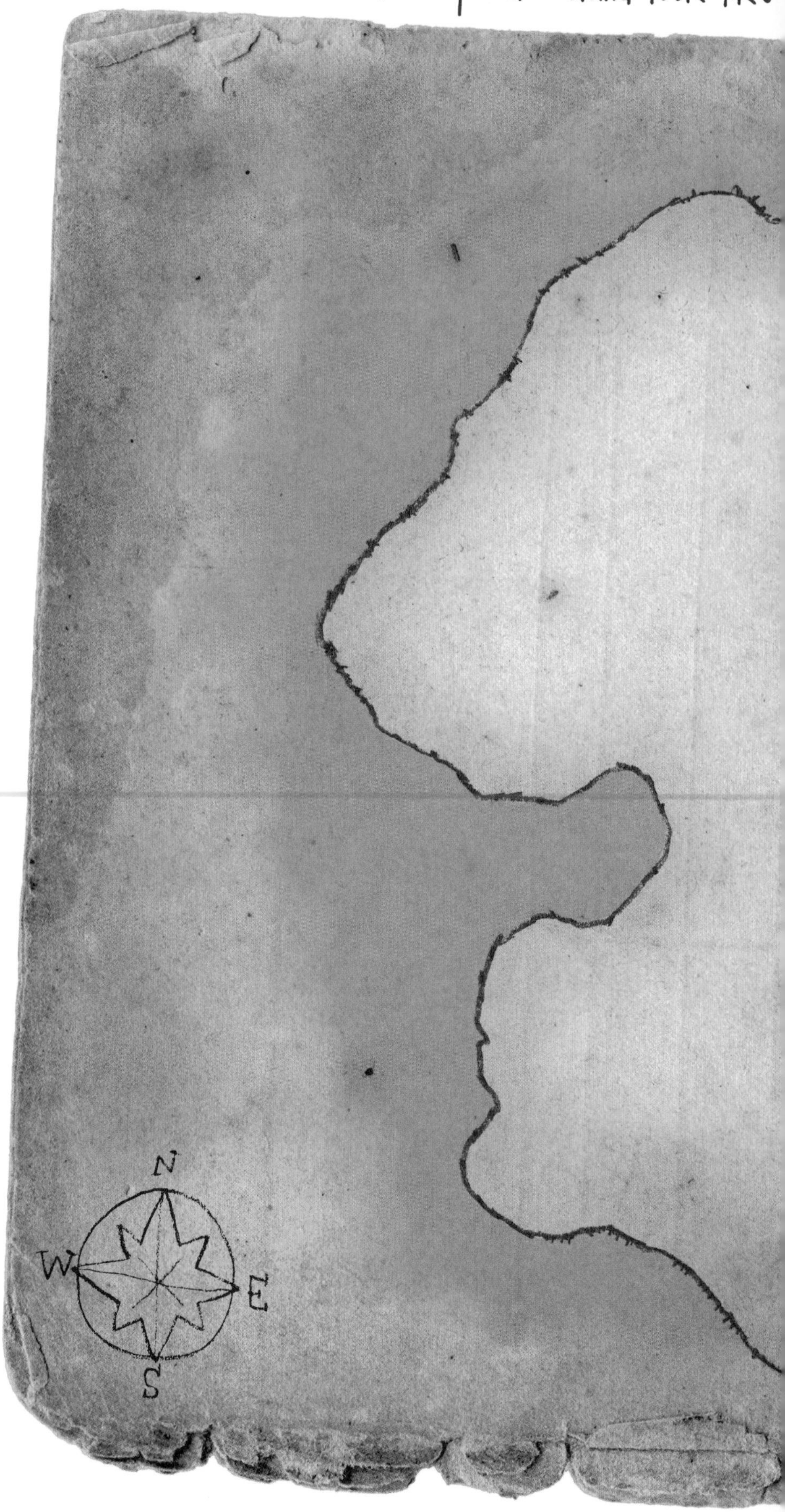

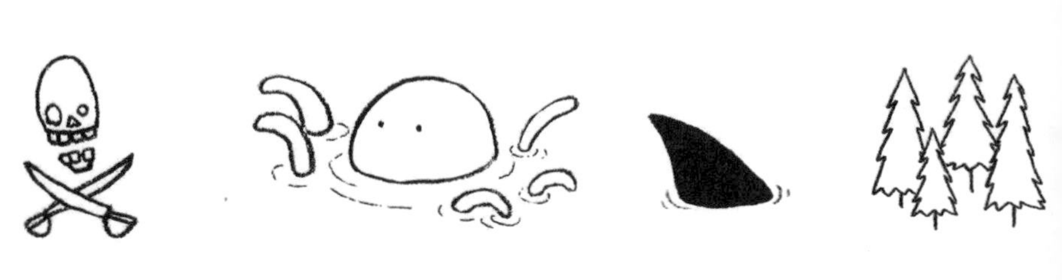

What designs can you add to this tea set?

What sort of city can you create by shading in the squares?

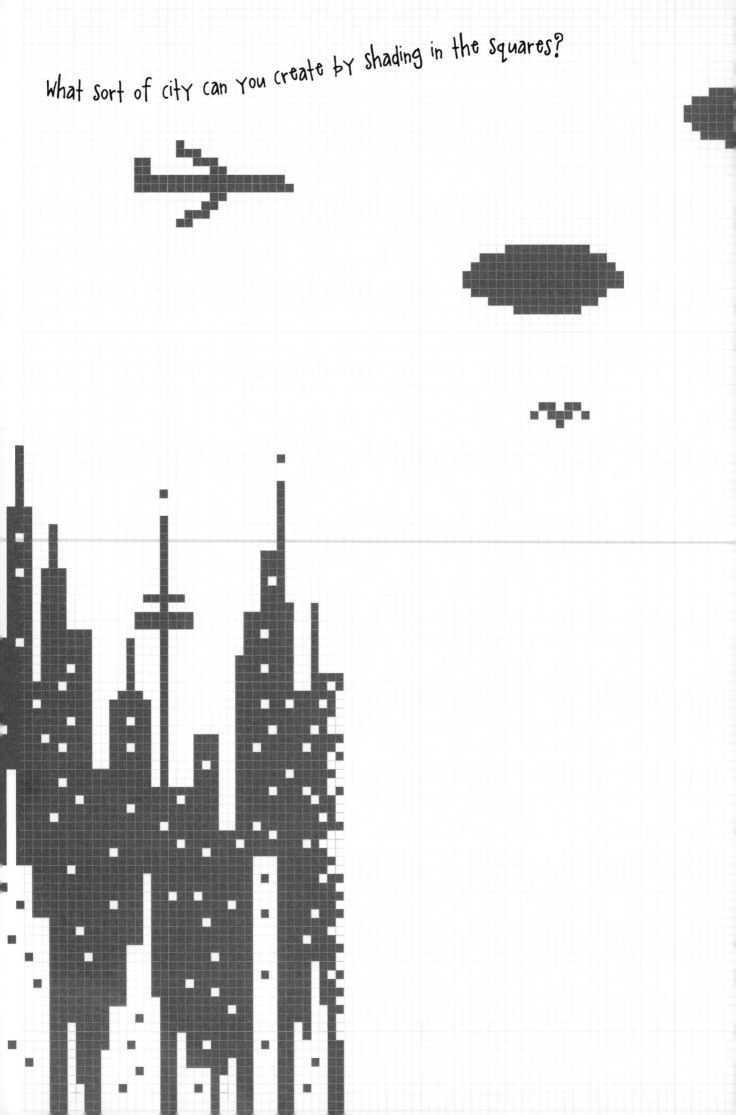

What has escaped from the zoo?

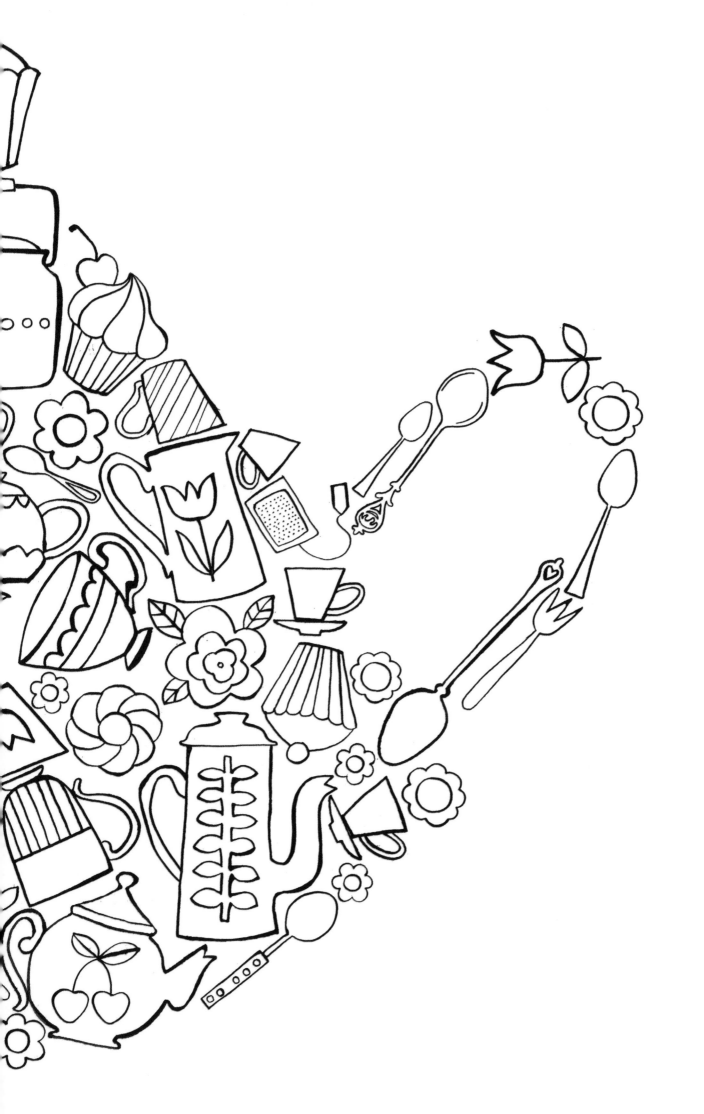

What awesome skateboard designs can you create?

What delicious flavours and toppings can you add to the cupcakes?

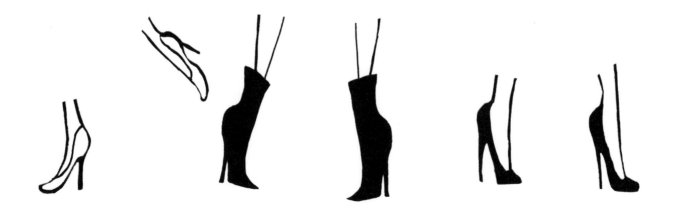

What sort of glamorous outfits are the fashion models wearing?

what do the gymnasts' swirling ribbons look like?

What shapes and colours can you add to fill the page?

What do your pet rocks look like?

CONTAINS 1 PUREBRED ROCK

this way UP

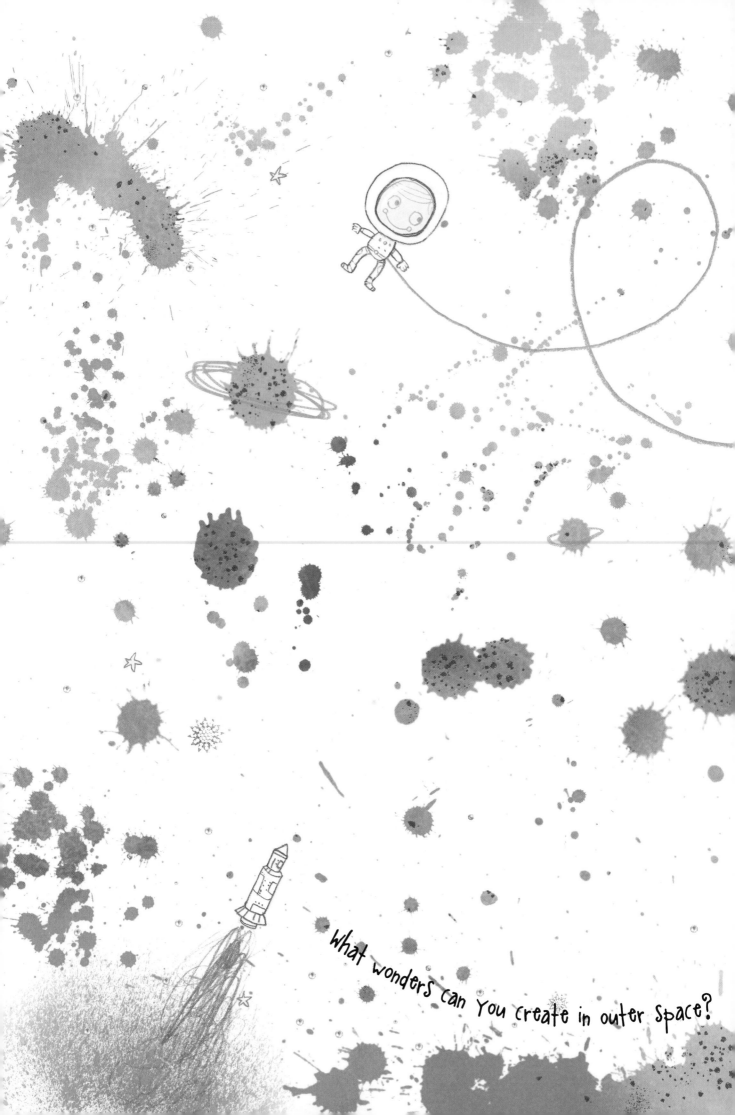

What wonders can you create in outer space?

☆ What does your rocket look like?

what do your rubber boots look like?

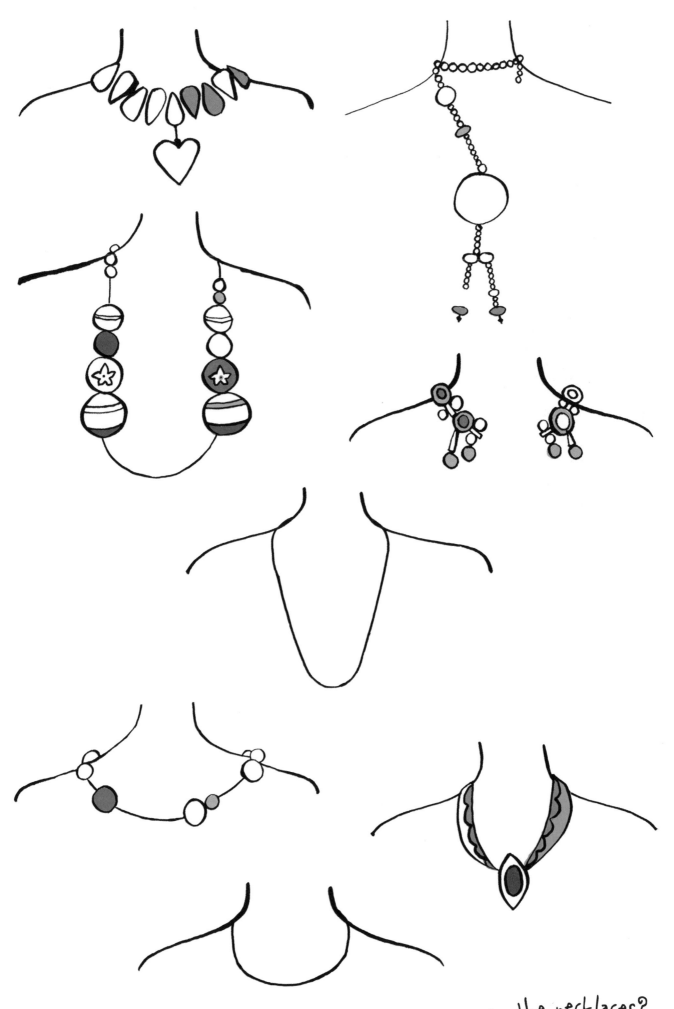

what beads and colours can you add to the necklaces?

WINTER

SPRING

SUMMER

AUTUMN

What do the trees in this forest look like during each season?

What amazing sights can be found in your city of the future?

what can you see in the x-ray machine?

What is in the vending machine?

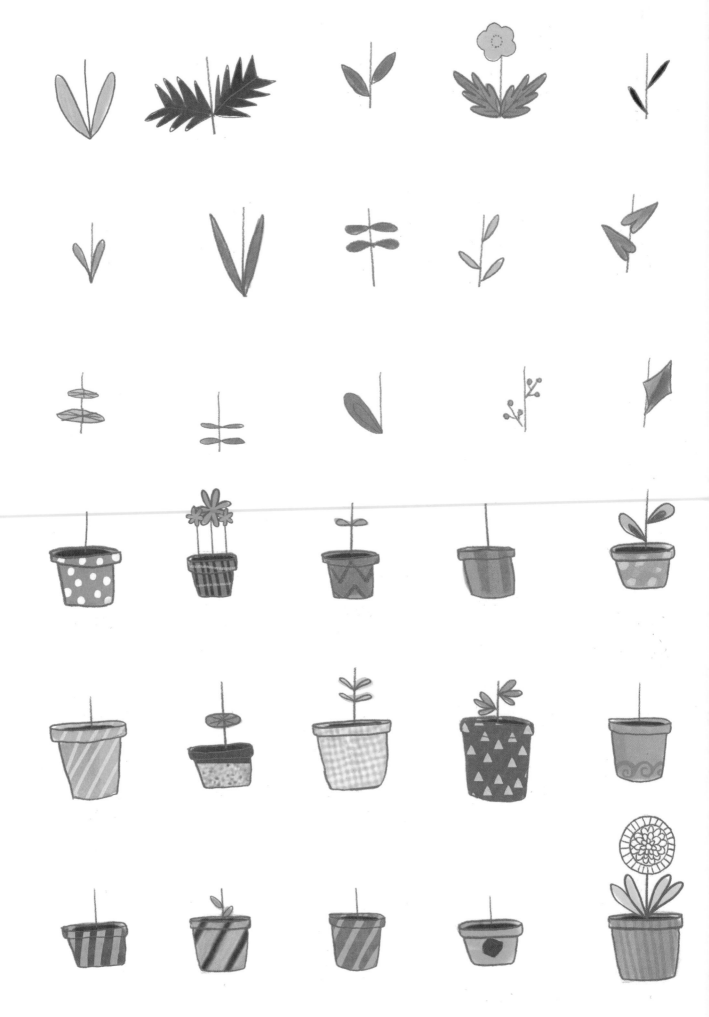

What sorts of flowers can you draw on the stalks and in the flowerpots?

what is at the top of the rope?

What do the tutus look like and what poses are your ballerinas making?

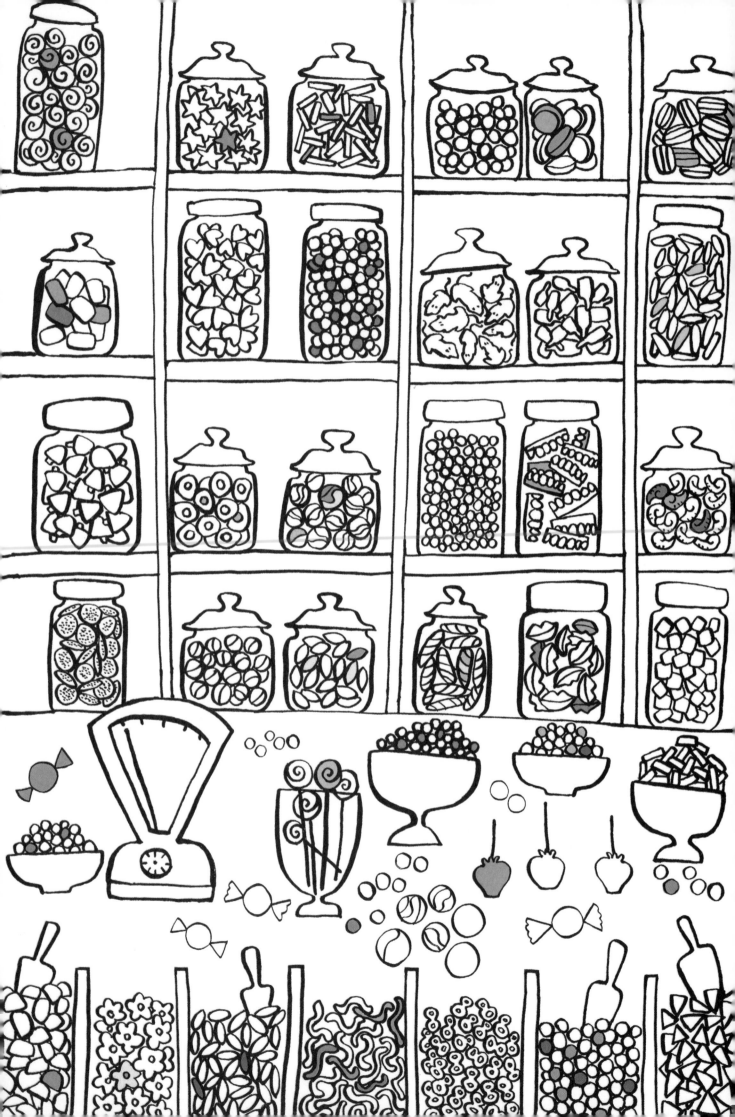

What patterns can you create in the bookmarks,
starting out simply and getting harder as you go?

What is happening on this stage?

What scary Halloween creatures can you create?

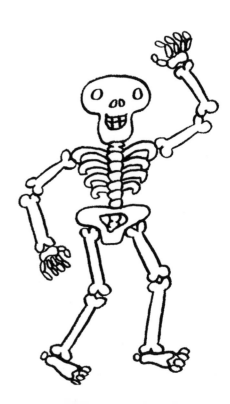

What varmint or critter is the cowboy lassoing?

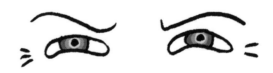

What faces can you create around these eyes?

What is everyone looking up at?

what does your ultimate birthday cake look like?

What delightful drawings can you create from these silly squiggles?

what patterns can you add to the nails?

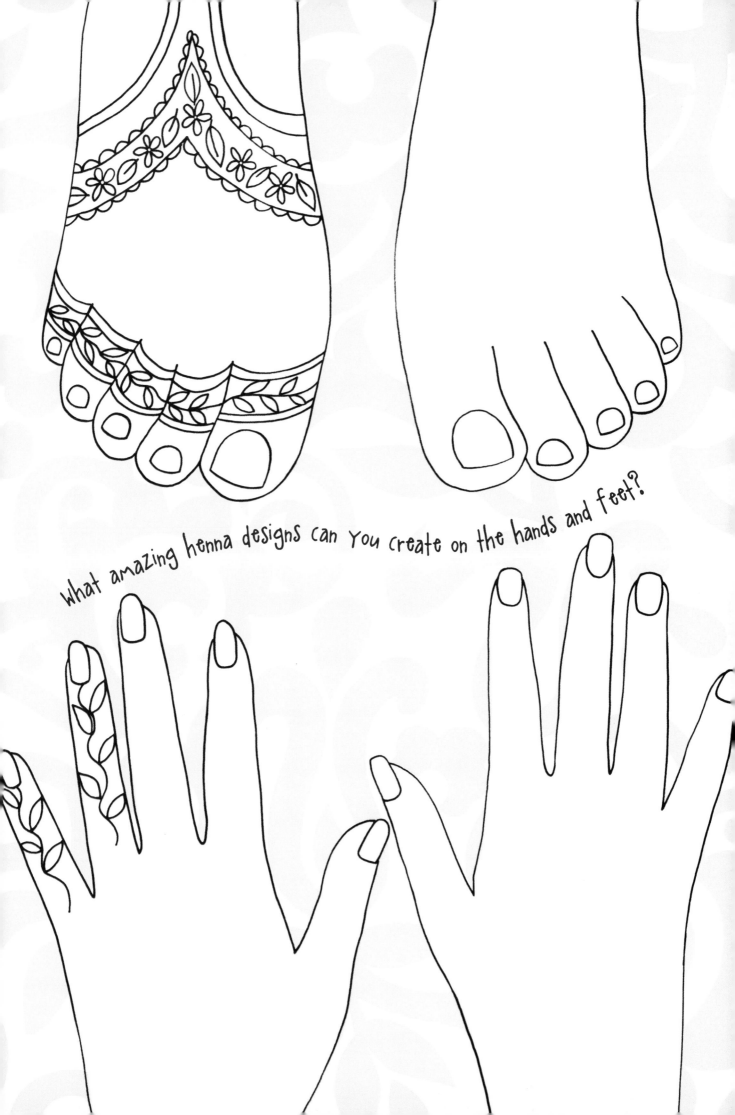

What amazing henna designs can you create on the hands and feet?

What can you create
from the clouds?

What is on TV?

What can be found in the broccoli forest?

What colours and patterns can you add to the stained-glass window?

Published by Hinkler Books Pty Ltd
45–55 Fairchild Street
Heatherton Victoria 3202 Australia
www.hinkler.com.au

h

hinkler

© Hinkler Books Pty Ltd 2013

Cover Design: Peter Tovey and
Hinkler Studio

Illustrations: by Mike Davidson,
Laura Hughes, Julie Ingham, Louise
Cunningham, Smiljana Coh and
Jess Golden

Prepress: Graphic Print Group

ISBN: 978 1 7435 2073 4

Printed and bound in China

Images © Shutterstock.com: Little cute chicky © waihoo;
Bulb © mhatzapa; Cartoon pencil © lineartestpilot;
Old rope © Art Allianz; ropes, Broken egg © Picsfive;
Stranded Boy, Photo of wrestler, Boy Posing Next To Fish,
Man Riding Ostrich © chippix; Shark © Nbenbow; Four
Children © Susan Law Cain; Wedding day © KUCO;
Photo-album © Zheltyshev; Fingerprints © charobnica;
Fingerprints © Undergroundarts.co.uk; Artificial toadstools
© Anneka; Four toadstools © Tomas Sereda; Old paper ©
Vitaly Korovin; Graph grid © optimarc; Collection Rocks
© xpixel; Cardboard box © Volodymyr Krasyuk; Pebbles
stones © nrt; Fresh Broccoli © Betacam-SP; Fresh broccoli
© yamix; broccoli © Adisa; Raw broccoli © Rene Jansa;
Broccoli vegetable © Nattika.